HARD DRIVE

Paul Stephenson studied modern languages and linguistics, then European studies. He has published three pamphlets: *Those People* (Smith/Doorstop, 2015), which won the Poetry Business pamphlet competition; *The Days that Followed Paris* (HappenStance, 2016), written after the November 2015 terrorist attacks; and *Selfie with Waterlilies* (Paper Swans Press, 2017). In 2013/14 he took part in the Jerwood/Arvon mentoring scheme and the Aldeburgh Eight, before completing the Poetry Business Writing School and pursuing an MA in Creative Writing (Poetry) with the Manchester Writing School. In 2018 he co-edited the 'Europe' issue of *Magma* (70) and since then has helped curate Poetry in Aldeburgh. He is a university teacher and researcher living between Cambridge and Brussels.

Hard Drive

Paul Stephenson

CARCANET POETRY

First published in Great Britain in 2023 by
Carcanet
Alliance House, 30 Cross Street
Manchester, M 2 7 A Q
www.carcanet.co.uk

A CIP catalogue record for this book is
available from the British Library.

ISBN 978 1 80017 327 8

Book design by Andrew Latimer & Paul Stephenson
Typesetting by BookLite, India

The publisher acknowledges financial
assistance from Arts Council England.

Supported using public funding by
ARTS COUNCIL
ENGLAND

CONTENTS

III. CLEARING SHELVES

IV. COVERED RESERVOIR

V. INTENTIONS

VI. ATTACHMENT

ANGLEPOISE

You'll be in the front room
at your computer,
surrounded by your family

of anglepoise lamps.
The novel will be making
steady progress.

I'll be in the kitchen
with my laptop and radio,
editing some poem or other,

devoting an hour to
the question of a comma,
semi-colon, full stop.

Voices will drift up to me
from where you are.
My drama will drift down

the hallway to you.
There'll be hot radiators
and rugs, curtains drawn.

We'll both be home,
absorbed in our projects,
each working our way

through the bottle of red.
I'll be alive. You'll be alive.
It'll be like old times.

HARD DRIVE

I. SIGNATURE

THE THESIS

It was June and I had to see a student.
A Tuesday morning and I had to see several students.
I knew something was wrong.
I called and asked a friend for help.
I was far away, and I had to see a student.

She said she'd go round and ring the bell.
I tried to listen to the mouth of the student.
He or she was seeking my approval.
I knew something was wrong.
It was June and I was seeing a student.

I gave some useful advice. I gave a smile.
I knew something was wrong.
I wished them well, saw off the student.
The deadline was approaching for submitting the thesis.
It was late morning and I had to see a student.

I sat across from a student, faced the thesis.
And then across from another student.
I waited for my friend's call. My friend was in London.
I knew something wasn't right.
I worked my way through the students.

WHAT JEAN SAW

Through the letterbox
the little bald patch of you
asleep on the floor

THE DESCRIPTION OF THE BUILDING

Online it says it's *homely in style*,
double-fronted and two-storied
with gable dormer windows in the roof.
It refers to brick quoins and brick surrounds,
two large chimneys, one either side,
and an arched entrance for large vehicles.

No reference is made to the red gloss
paint of the door, or to the red gloss
of the gates to the right. It doesn't talk about
the sign: *No parking – Gates in Constant Use*,
or how the red acts as a beacon for visitors
when the day is turning overcast.

It talks about a plaque from 1891
by the Hackney District Board of Works,
and how the place played a crucial role
in 'Operation Mincemeat', informed
the international non-fiction bestseller
The Man Who Never Was.

A lengthy text, it doesn't mention how,
when you've an appointment to see the body,
you stare over at the building
from inside the car, muttering *That must be it*,
while the driver, a family member
or close friend, roots around for change.

SIGNATURE

In his sleep, except he isn't
really sleeping (that's just what we
like to tell ourselves), he looks as if he's
grinning, as if he knows something new,
has seen a sight to comfort him and
offer reassurance so he can close
his eyes for good. Or else he's understood,
once and for all, what us lot don't
that this here is one massive joke,
some lame farce from the beginning.
I wouldn't be surprised, because he has,
because he had, his own sense of humour,
black, in the mishaps and embarrassment
saw the human comedy, relishing
the doddering and stumbling of others,
their sticky situations, how they keep on
talking, talking, words making it worse,
digging a hole for themselves. I look
at his mouth and he's not saying much
but keeping shtum, lips sealed, mum's
the word. And I am positive, one hundred
per cent, that he won't tell me what is
tickling him, not this time. I edge up, lean in
and steep over, allow myself to touch his
forehead, lay my palm flat on the long fringe
and with my thumb caress each fine brow,
stroke them in the right direction, feel the love
cold and wet from refrigeration.

I TELL HIM ABOUT THE PEOPLE

who have been in touch, about
his parents, my brother, Mum and Tom,
the friends we've not seen in years,
the ones we spent good times with,
drinking and laughing, gallivanting.

I want him to hear how we've been
in contact, keen for him to know
they're all thinking of him. I need him
to learn, one by one, the long list
of our life, of all those who love him.

In a hushed tone, speaking softly,
sorry for my silly embarrassment,
paranoid in case someone's there –
a mortuary worker listening
from behind the curtain backdrop,

I stand in the low-ceilinged room
and force myself, try to keep it casual,
muster words to fill the quiet.
I run out of names, exhaust the list,
resort to love and apologies.

include the Thracian Gladiator, Spartacus
and Roman Emperor, Lucius Verus

include the painter, Caravaggio
and the painter, Dora Carrington

include the composer, George Gershwin
and the composer, Felix Mendelssohn

include the novelist, Charlotte Brontë
and the novelist, Mary Wollstonecraft

include the poet, Federico García Lorca
and the poet, Guillaume Apollinaire

include Charles II of Spain
and Louis XVI of France

include William, Prince of Orange
and King Oswald of Northumbria

MY MONARCH

In his gown of white cotton with intricate brocade,
here he lies, collected and regal, my own medieval

King of England

He'd like that, *of England*, this his adopted country,
lying in a white cotton gown with intricate brocade.

His nose is finer than I recall, cheeks a little sunken.
Hair beneath the chin, like he's missed a bit shaving.

Up to his chest, a dark purple velvet with gold trim.
He lies here in white cotton, the intricate brocade.

APERTURE (WINTER POEM)

~~This morning, red sky through a sash window,~~
~~a sloping glass roof and frosted path curving.~~

~~I didn't venture out but instead took a photo,~~
~~to freeze time and to capture the moment.~~

~~A camera is a remarkable thing, how it preserves~~
~~what we see. Or later, invites us to look again.~~

> *Some people like to take a photo,*
> said the woman in the mortuary.

I would never have dreamed of taking a photo.
No sound, no flash, he took one, took several.

An innocent act. I will not forget the taking.
A camera is a phone is a knot in my stomach.

I hate the viewfinder and I hate the focus.
I hate the shutter release, the way light bounces.

HUMOROUS ELBOWINGS
after Elizabeth Bishop 'The Bight'

Humorous elbowings, not serious ones.
Not dour elbowings that started the day
on the wrong arm. Elbowings that can
see what's funny, elbowings that rib you,
tickle your sides. No sour-faced elbowings.
No no-nonsense elbowings, just elbowings
that don't nudge, that aren't dead or dying
but deadpan. That category of elbowings
with a glisten in their joint, those that love
to really take the mickey out of kneeings.
Elbowings that don't do diets or obsess
over headlines or sorting the recycling or
train for years of evening classes to qualify
as Tax Accountants. Elbowings that crack
blue jokes like eggs producing blue chicks
whose blue runs off in the rain. Elbowings
you can trust in a crowd and know will
pay back every single penny. Elbowings
that conduct live orchestras to an absent
audience and take a modest bow. Elbowings
that walk the aisle counting to themselves
calmly before take-off. Elbowings tucked in
beneath a sheet and ready for the flight.

MASTERPIECE THEATRE

Standing there, I peer up into corners of the ceiling,
check for CCTV, a pinhole camera or discreet lens,
some hidden device in place to catch my gullibility.

This has to be a stunt, an overgrown student prank,
each whisper, each tear for public entertainment.
With that tight grin, I wouldn't put it past you.

What is this, a black comedy laid on just for me?
So you're playing your part. Am I saying my piece,
on cue, with my improvised script of not much?

I say goodbye, and one last touch, my legs moving
towards the door. In the instant, I turn, see your head
tilt towards me, your eyes blinking open, staring back.

NOT DEAD

I.

You could have given me a heart attack. The lights came on,
a white blinding light, and the walls of the room fell like flaps.
Behind your body, the dark curtain was pulled back to reveal
a swell of people one hundred across and forty rows high
who clapped and cheered and stood up from their seats.
I could feel the heat of the spotlights on my neck and back.

Cameras on runners rushed in like medics and the boom
was lowered to catch the sound of me rasping, me trying
to catch my breath. The show host ran over, beckoning you
out from beneath your perfectly tucked-in, crisp, white sheet.
His shiny assistants whipped it back, carried you over so
he could show us off, his arms wrapped round our shoulders.

And when he let go and drew back, I wanted to thump you
but instead squeezed you so hard I could count your heart
and buried my head in your chest and wept, and the truth
crumbled onto the blue linoleum of the hangar-like studio
from where you were transmitting and I was broadcasting
to the whole nation. We were on air together, going live.

2.

During the commercial break we sat in the green room
on an orange sofa and drank champagne, raising a toast
to artifice and then a toast to your impressive acting skills
and ability for deception and you set about telling me how
you'd been planning it all for weeks. You beamed and I
suggested we go celebrate with a slap-up meal in Soho.

Let's go you said, drinking up, grabbing your usual khaki
rucksack and off we went, Piccadilly Line (the TV studio
was out in Zone 5). We queued for a while, got a corner table,
ate our fill. It was better than ever as you fed me every detail
from the books you'd borrowed from the London Library,
all you'd learnt about trickery, on stillness and mis-seeing.

It was chilly for June. We walked fast to Euston, ended up
up top of the 143 to Crouch End which was empty and slow,
us exhausted from excitement, but it didn't matter because
you were you again and I was me. The next day was normal,
nothing special. We slept in late. Lazy day. Weather bleurgh.
You were a bit depressed as usual, and I popped out for milk.

Tod – *noun (1)*: a male fox, a dog, a reynard; a fox, chiefly in Scotland; example, 'the *tod*, or fox, is their totem, and him they diligently pursue'; *tod*, someone like a fox, a crafty person; *noun (2)* archaic, an English unit of weight for wool, one equal to 28 pounds or 12.7 kilograms but varying locally; *noun (3)*, a load, a clump, a bushy mass, especially of ivy; *noun (4)*: meaning death, or cessation of life; *noun (5)* used in the British expression: *on one's tod* meaning to be on one's own, originating in nineteenth century rhyming slang from *Tod Sloan/alone*, after *Tod* Sloan, a jockey; *word origin:* from the Middle English *todd, todde*; akin to the Old High German *zotta*, meaning tuft of hair; to the East Frisian dialect, *todde*, for rag or small load; or to the Old Norse, *toddi*, meaning piece or slice; *tod*, apparently cognate with the Starland Frisian *todde*, meaning bundle; else the Swedish *todd*, a mass of wool; *verb*: *to tod*, now obselete, meaning to weigh, to yield in tods; third-person singular simple present, he/she *tods*; present participle, *todding*; simple past and past participle, he/she *todded;* also found in place names: Todmorden, a Yorkshire market town at the confluence of three valleys; El-Tod, a village and archaeological site in Egypt; Mount Tod, in British Columbia, Canada, also Mount Tod near Amundsen Bay, Antarctica; commercial name: *TOD*, a luxury brand of leather shoes and handbags; in aviation, acronym of the term *top of descent*; trade name for a vehicle four-wheel drive system *torque on demand*; *Tournament of Death*, an annual professional wrestling event; *Türkiye Ormancilar Derneği*, the Foresters' Association of Turkey; *tod*, anagram of *dot*, as in *dot-to-dot*, a numbered drawing game for children; English words containing *tod*: today, toddle off, toddy; foreign words containing *tod*: in German, *das Tod* (death), *der Todesangst* (a fear of dying); in Dutch, *Todo*, contraction of *toegevoegd docent* (additional teacher); in Spanish, *todos* (everyone), *todo* (everything), *en todas partes* (everywhere).

CONDDOLENCES

If I receive yet another message of sympathy
with your name spelled incorrectly with two *d*'s

I'll go and find a very large puddle and carry
a stepladder over, place it right in the middle,

climb up and huddle. I'll do my goddamndest
to look forbidding to the befuddled grandaddy

doddering along, and to the downtrodden daddies
in shiny caddies driving their kiddies and goddess

wives to work at rush hour. I won't scream or
redden but be meddlesome, twiddle my fingers

and do diddly squat. I'll sit and cuddle myself,
wee myself, widdling and piddling like a toddler

in a muddle, like a middle-aged *Manneken Pis*
in the saddle on high having a long Jimmy Riddle.

GRIEF, IT'S NOT WHAT IT USED TO BE

cos it used to be gravel
flicked up by a spinning car tyre
that punctured your heart.
Used to be a hungry Gruffalo
that flattened you when you
went for a walk. We're talking

weeks deep in a grotto
with underground lakes, nothing
but the drumming of stalactite
drips drilling into your head.
Back then it was the Garbo
of all Garbos: *I want to be alone*

forever, a gruelling Greek
tragedy in three thousand acts.
It used to be Day Four
and gripped by sorrow, the desire
to drown yourself ungraciously
at Hampton Court Lock.

THE FRACTION LEFT OVER IS LARGE

On a scale of one to your dying
I'm somewhere in the middle.

Eight out of ten of your deaths
were never worked out.

Half of you dead is more than
the half of me alive.

94 per cent of respondents said 'Sorry'
and 6 per cent didn't answer.

None of you replied.
100 per cent of you did not respond.

II. OFFICIALDOM

VOICEMAIL

Sarah is away next week so would like to speak to me
today if it's convenient and not too much trouble.
She wants to go over some of the finer details
and explain how things will generally go from here.

Sarah needs to check she's understood correctly
and revisit a few points so we can move the process on.
She'd like us to consider the options together and
ensure I'm fully informed re decisions to be made.

Sarah says a number of procedures must be got underway,
that she should be in touch asap with the necessary parties.
Sarah tells me one or two loose ends need tying up
before she leaves the office for a fortnight's holiday.

Sarah has written me an email to this effect on Monday.
She is thankful and looks forward to talking with me.
Sarah hopes to hear from me, this afternoon, preferably,
and would be very grateful if I'd return her call.

OFFICIALDOM

This case file
is not *concerning*.

It is not *about*.
It does not *regard*.

This case file
is not *relating to*

or *pertaining to*
the matter in hand.

This case file is *touching*
the death of

and like a forefinger
on the lips,

I am touched
by its usage, how

it seeks to soften
what is so hard.

INTERROGATIVE

'And so how did he die?' they say,
'…if you don't mind me asking.'

'Well, the…' he hesitates, surprised,
confused by the motive to the question.

'I don't mean to be nosey,' they assure,
smiling politely and stepping back.

'Erm, all I…' he utters, '…it's just that,'
unsure if he really knows for certain.

'I was just wondering if…' they continue,
saying 'Sorry I don't mean to pry…'

'Ignore me,' they say, 'engage brain
before opening mouth, and all that…'

'No, it's fine,' he insists, 'really, it's fine,
…it's a perfectly reasonable question.'

THE TRAIN TO SÓLLER

what a view   my god what a view   my god what a view   my god what
it was   I don't think it was   I don't think it was   I don't think
and shake   the rattle and shake   the rattle and shake   the rattle
could see   I wish you could see   I wish you could see   I wish you
up high   that peak there up high   that peak there up high   that peak
down below   the green down below   the green down below   the green

here I know   you're still here I know   you're still here I know   you're
tunnel won't end   this tunnel won't end   this tunnel won't end   this
why did you go   but why did you go   but why did you go   but why
and so wide   so steep and so wide   so steep and so wide   so steep
on the ledge   propped proud on the ledge   propped proud on the
two   the tickets for two   the tickets for two   the tickets

the cold   to hold back the cold   to hold back the cold   to hold back
the pine   the palm plane and pine   the palm plane and pine   the palm
on the floor   asleep on the floor   asleep on the floor   asleep on the
sight   spectacular sight   spectacular sight   spectacular
blue   the clear sky deep blue   the clear sky deep blue   the clear
other signs   but no other signs   but no other signs   but no

CAUSE (2016)

Soft heart failure / Hard heart failure / Short, sharp heart failure / Rich heart failure / Poor heart failure / Clean heart failure / Blind heart failure / Red, white and blue heart failure / Smooth heart failure / Green heart failure / Fast heart failure / Slow heart failure / Bold heart failure / Frictionless heart failure / Furtive heart failure / Transitional heart failure / Canada-style heart failure / Norway plus heart failure / No deal heart failure / Ukraine-style heart failure / Unlawful heart failure / Swiss heart failure / Turkish heart failure / Australian heart failure / Exact same benefits heart failure / Tariff-free heart failure / Flaccid heart failure / Jobs first heart failure / Proud heart failure / Full English heart failure / Dog's breakfast heart failure / Chaotic heart failure / Bespoke heart failure / Have your cake and eat it heart failure / In name only heart failure / Schrödinger's heart failure / Smart heart failure / Titanic heart failure / Train crash heart failure / Cliff edge heart failure / Crème brûlée heart failure / Global heart Failure / Reverse heart failure / Oven-ready heart failure

GRIEF AS TWO SIDES OF THE ATLANTIC OCEAN

This side me. That side them.
This side ten o'clock. That side five.

This side work. That side retirement.
This side students. That side antiques.

This side mobile. That side cell.
This side pub. That side bar.

This side Centigrade. That side Fahrenheit.
This side window. That side aircon.

This side post mortem. That side autopsy.
This side aeroplane. That side airplane.

This side mash. That side grits.
This side stone. That side pounds.

This side pan. That side skillet.
This side shops. That side stores.

This side licence. That side license.
This side pills. That side drugs.

This side jug. That side pitcher.
This side duvet. That side comforter.

This side autumn. That side fall.
This side harbours. That side harbors.

This side getting on with it. That side too.
This side telling everyone. That side no one.

MISTAKE

Gone one on leaving.
We went for lunch.
Some random Mexican.
No idea how we managed
refried beans and guacamole.

She'd wanted to see him,
come over to see him,
so I took her to see him.
It had been a fortnight
since I'd first seen him.

Wish I hadn't arranged it.
Wish we hadn't gone.
She was in a state and I was
horrified by time,
what two weeks could do.

We talked and we ate.
Even talked about other things.
Then we paid the bill,
and she took the bus
and I took the Tube.

THE BUTTON

Michael appeared, just as he said he would. He issued
hushed words with a soft Irish accent, his demeanour
tidy, calm, professional, familiar. We had to get going –
someone was after us, so it couldn't run over. Michael
just wanted to talk through a few last details including
the button. The button. There, next to the wooden lectern.
He guided me over. *Would you like me to take care of it?*
Or when we got to the final song, would I be up to it?

Could I bring myself to take care of the button? He'd be
on hand, standing at the rear of the chapel. Looking back,
I don't know how I pushed it, or if he said to *push* or *press*
or what verb, if the button was green like 'green for go',
green as the pool table lawn, or red, red as the brick arches
and spent roses, or was it black? Why did I push it? Push
because I was a crazed control freak that July Tuesday,
me playing at master of ceremonies? Or was it out of duty?

The button, I mean. For it was silly, like an am-dram prop.
Though the button was small, it was also violent and, oh, I
shouldn't have been allowed to make a person disappear
with such a tiny weapon. O, it was horrid in its automation,
melodramatic and almost camp, yes, that's it, it was camp!
Vulgar and hammed up, a tasteless step, banal, extravagant.
Which was apt, in an affected sort of way, because T would
likely have pressed it himself, acting out a theatrical ruse.

It's just, if nobody had pushed the button, the huge curtain
wouldn't have wrapped round and I'd never have caught
a corner glance of the doors parting, letting in a sharp slit
of white light as he was taken. He'd have lain there, *in situ*,
our modest gathering filing out into the midday sunshine
and I'd be even more a mess, knowing I'd not sent him off
completely, beneath that bed of summer flowers I flung on
as they carried him in, a meadow all orange, purple, all yellow.

THE HYMN OF HIM

The app of him, the bop of him, the cap,
      the cop of him, the cup of him, the dip;
the fop of him, the gap of him, the hip,
      the hop of him, the jip of him, the lap.

The lip of him, the map of him, the mop,
      the nap of him, the nip of him, the pep;
the pip of him, the pup of him, the quip,
      the rap of him, the rep of him, the rip.

The sap of him, the sip of him, the sup,
      the tap of him, the tip of him, the top;
the VIP of him, the whip of him, the yap,
      the yep of him, the zap of him, the zip.

The ship of him, the shop of him, the sh'up,
      the chap of him, the chip of him, the chop.

RETORT

I knew *retort* was a sharp remark,
typically, a clever and witty reply,
could hear the angry accusation:
I just don't know you anymore!

I thought it a kind of retaliation,
cutting riposte, defensive rebuke –
caught the snapping back:
Yeah right, like you ever really did!

I took it as means of repayment
for insult, a wound with words,
had no notion of cremation:
the chamber, its heat-resistant bricks.

A TONIC OF STONES

Ones you stumble across, right there looking stony.
Humble stones, standing alone. Take stones in Umbria

where summer intones without umbrellas. Stonking stones
drunk on sun, in their oneness stunned, a stone stoned.

Stones like nests for pebbles that revel in the stonic quality
of their cold. Your toes reading out sentences of stones,

hitting low notes of stones, soles flat and stoical on a senate
of stones, palms stocking up for windowsills, paperweights.

Nasty stones. Oiks of grey and unrounded. Stones of undone.
Onus on stones. On tonnes. On tonnes to stones. Stonnets.

COLLECTING YOU FROM GOLDERS GREEN

The young woman / lady / female
behind the desk / counter / reception
spoke gently / softly / calmly
seemed genuinely moved / emotional / upset
and I thought how generous / kind / ridiculous
for she never knew / met / was acquainted with / you

She checked her screen / monitor / computer
and vanished / took her leave / was gone
I sat on the sofa / couch / settee
looking / staring / glancing / around the office
at the pot plant / cheese plant / cactus
until she came back / returned / reappeared

She was holding / carrying / balancing
a large / sizeable / ample / brown
container / receptacle / cardboard box
neatly / immaculately / pristinely / sealed
with your name / surname / identifier
on a white label / sticker / square / in jet black

I got in the car / vehicle / motor
and sat / positioned / placed / you
safely on my knees / legs / lap
I felt the weight / pounds / load / of you
as Jean drove / escorted / chauffeured / me
away / to Highgate / to hers / home

NAMESAKE
after Nicolas Tredell

Tod not Todorov. Tod not Tzvetan, son of Todor Todorov Borov and Haritian (née Peeva) Todorova. Tod not Todorov. Not born in Sofia, capital of Bulgaria, a one-party communist state from 1946 to 1989. Tod not Todorov. Not with an attitude of detachment from political and social issues. Tod not Todorov. No desire to avoid the dogmas of communist literary criticism. Not inclined towards a formalist approach to literary study. Tod not Todorov. Not graduating from the University of Sofia in 1961. Not heading to Paris in 1963 at the age of twenty-four to pursue a doctorate with a soon-to-be famous supervisor, Roland Barthes. Tod not Todorov. Not a yet-to-become French citizen with ample time for research and writing, without the obligation to teach. Tod not Todorov. Not deploying his knowledge of Russian. And not translating into French esoteric and elusive formalist texts. Tod not Todorov. Never co-founding the influential journal *Poétique* in 1970, which promoted formalist and structuralist literary theory and analysis. Not Todorov but Tod. Preferring prose. Into letterpress type, wooden printing blocks. Fancying fonts. Not Todorov but Tod. Spending teenage summers in Romania, a school year in Lewes. Not Todorov but Tod. Liking frogs. Middle name Greenfield, gift from his mother. Tod not Tod.

LETTER FROM AMERICA

And now your mother writes,
says she's been fighting the groundhog.
She tells me she sits in wait,
watches the groundhog as it comes
trampling everything.

She's been keeping busy
and put up a makeshift fence,
shooting at the ground with her BB gun
even though it's strictly illegal
to discharge weapons in the borough.

She's more than willing to take a chance
where the groundhog's concerned.
And so she watches, watches it waddle,
a symbol of where she's living.
Summer goes on, hot and humid.

A PRAYER FOR DEATH ADMIN

For the message received to establish contact
and being the designated representative;
For the formal letter of authorization
and acting on behalf in matters regarding.

For the considerable information to take on board
and the tissue samples to be carefully taken
(approximately the size of a thumbnail);
For the detailed microscope examination.

For the offer of assistance with all legalities
and the certified copies for permanent filing;
For the attached information sheet to be completed
and the ten copies (but more if requested).

For the confirmation of cancelled subscription
and the 40 pounds refunded to a credit card;
For the stop to collection activity on the account
and the number to please quote in all correspondence.

For the utility companies: E.ON, EDF, First Utility
and their written request for meter readings;
For their final statements of accurate usage
and music placed on hold with Virgin Media.

For the clearing of contents, bulk waste collection
and the end of tenancy move out cleaning;
For the follow-up note that card transactions will appear
on your bank statement as: FANTASTIC SERVICES.

For the automated replies to emails received successfully
(and passed on to the appropriate council department);
For the aim to make things as smooth as possible for you
and the paid-up start date for postal redirection.

For the message entitled: 'Death of a library user'
and the titles of the six books currently issued;
For the overdue fines waived (no further fees accruing)
and the reassurance not to worry if you can't locate them.

III. CLEARING SHELVES

BATTLESHIPS

I must sort his room, a room as full
of ships as any room could be, clear up
the battle waging on open seas.

I imagine them, christened one summer afternoon,
careering down their slipway,
ironclad onto polished parquet.

Red and blue ships strewn – mile-long,
laden with guided missiles,
locked onto my feet, closing in on my knees.

Picking up a ship, I cup it, poor target,
slide a knife in the cracks
between floorboards to extricate others.

No mayday for these navies in trouble,
these heavily manned fleets,
their broadsides struck, hulls torn and listing.

For the scuttled and sunk, damaged
and wrecked, the ships reported missing,
I bag them up and think charity.

No more games here.
No more torpedoes in crossfire – hit!
His room a tidy horizon, the radar blank.

CLEARING HIS SHELVES

Foreign Affairs Pacific Agony Over There
The System of Objects Public Enemies The Brief and Awesome Reign of Phil
States of Desire Good Morning, Midnight Meanings of the Market
The God Delusion L'Histoire de France Think Like a Champion!

The Private Life of Chairman Mao The Eccentricities of Cardinal Pirelli

Love Lasts Three Years Here is Where We Meet Pleasure in the Eighteenth Century
Interesting Times The State We're In Sweet Tooth
Graphs, Maps, Trees A Theatre of Human Nature Enduring Creation
Mapping the Heavens Rhymed Ruminations Language and Solitude

The Master Builder and Other Plays The Rise of the Russian Consumer

Art & Illusion The Life of Oscar Wilde The View From Africa
What Young Men Do The Group The Assassin
The History of Human Marriage Vol. 1 The History of Human Marriage Vol. 2
The History of Human Marriage Vol. 3 The Jungle Trouble in Paradise

The Playboy of the Western World Bedouin of the London Evening

The Silent Traveller The Four-Gated City More Green Fingers
The Day it Rained Forever The Days Before Yesterday Bouvard and Pécuchet
The Worst-Case Scenario Cities of the Interior Vol .1 Cities of the Interior Vol. 2
Who was That Man? The Wayfarer Summer in Williamsburg

The Notebooks of Don Rigoberto The Mortgaged Heart

THE ONLY BOOK I TOOK

I.

The Year of Magical Thinking.
Hadn't read it, knew you liked it.
Hardback edition. Alfred A. Knopf.

227 pages. Copyright © 2005.
The dust jacket intact, mint green spine.
The back cover quote reads:

Life changes fast.
Life changes in the instant.
You sit down to dinner and life as you know it ends.

II.

Flick to the first page
and there it is, that quote again –
now with a fourth line:

Life changes fast.
Life changes in the instant.
You sit down to dinner and life as you know it ends.
The question of self-pity.

What's wrong with self-pity?
Is it not commercial enough?
Would it put off the buying public?

III.

A handsome bookmark inside
from WONDER BOOK with a flash sign
that says 'Share the Wonder'

and 'If we have earned
a 5 don't forget to leave * * * * *
5.0 out of 5.0 Feedback'

'Less than 5 is not
nearly good enough for our valued customers!'
Did you leave any feedback?

YOUR NOVEL
after Luke Kennard

is such a brilliant idea. When I hear you're still working on it
I'm so relieved. Not because you might have ditched it but
because it's not been published, not yet, after all these years of
you doing nothing but working on it. Full-time. I couldn't be
more reassured to learn you're suffering from writer's block,
spending the days reading around instead, and I must confess,
I've repeated to others with glee all about your repetitive strain
injury, giggled to myself at your carpal tunnel. Your appetite
for accuracy paralyses you and this electrifies me. It's important
to be authentic but not as important as rewriting your first
chapter thirty-two times until it's almost there. When I
inquire, feigning interest, and you tell me excitedly that you're
on a roll and impress me with your latest Word Count, I feel
panicked and think about wiping your hard drive, consider
breaking in with a torch at four am in search of your backup
files which I'll throw into a skip in the neighbouring street
where they're having a basement games room dug out. But not
before jumping up and down on it first in my heavy winter
shoes. When we meet for coffee after your writing group and
you run their new suggestions by me and admit you're not sure
whether to ignore them or incorporate them, totally or in part,
I shout *Incorporate, incorporate!* in a frenzy, all for every one
of them, not doubting for an instant, as if non-incorporation
were life-threatening, and hoping you will ruminate over the
feedback in an old beige cardigan with elbow pads whose
threads are loose, and then start pulling it all apart, cutting and
pasting large chunks of text into new Word documents you'll
forget where you've saved. I feel like a million dollars when you
go off on a tangent about a Mongolian mountain gradient and
start googling inclines, insist that this is crucial to the setting.
I'm jubilant when you say the three interspersing, unreliable

narrators and the subtle-but-not-too-subtle parallels with a far-off small country we all love to ridicule, plus your newly dreamt-up surprise plot twist, have all the makings of a stronger, more exciting and original bestseller, though a literary one, one that will be lauded in the *Times Literary Supplement* and *London Review of Books*, not on sale at airports. I tell you how much I'm loving what I hear and my face lights up as if with respect for your erudition, your prodigious talent, and I can hear myself urging you to keep going, to keep at it, each and every day, sympathizing that, yes it's a slog and, yes, you're in it for the long haul, because it's all about delayed gratification, even if there are days when you can only manage a hundred words, which is still something, because you must know, have a sense of the glory and prizes to come, and that one day soon it will have all been worth it.

CLINICALLY PROVEN

I take your face creams.
They're in the bathroom drawer.
Some empty, some on the go.

Your Regenerist ® Serum for Neck and Jawline from ® Olay
Your Regenerist ® 3-Point Super Firming Serum from ® Olay
Your Regenerist ® Micro-Sculpting Cream™ from ® Olay

Your Revitalift ® Concentrated Serum from L'Oréal ® Paris
Your Revitalift ® Miracle Blur Oil-Free Instant Skin Smoother from L'Oréal ® Paris
Your Revitalift ® Double Lifting Day/Jour Moisturizer from L'Oréal ® Paris
Your Revitalift ® Triple Power Day and Night Cream from L'Oréal ® Paris
Your Revitalift ® Broad Spectrum SPF20 Sunscreen from L'Oréal ® Paris

Your Men Expert™ Vita Lift Lifting Moisturizer with Intense Double Action
Pro-Tensium and Pro-Retinol Two in One Firming Gel + Anti-Wrinkle Cream from
L'Oréal ® Paris

You should see my face.
It's so smooth.
The *éclat*. The glow.

BIRKENSTOCKS

Your sandals used to irk me – the way
they showcased your two big toes and
wide, flat feet. Comfortable, I'm sure,
but for my taste, too much foot on display.
This morning I was on their website,
read all about tradition and ethos,
how they're crafted, made from a mix
of latex and leather, felt and jute.
I wondered at the season's bestsellers:
Mayari in metallic rose, pearl or yellow
and *Cameron*, the whacky silver model.
Yours were the classic, always *Arizona*,
dark brown, two straps, brass buckles.
I watched the video – in German, scrolled
down to learn about cork, how oak trees
are worked in strict rotation, the bark lifted
every nine years like peeling a new skin.
They gave long close-ups of the hands
of the Portuguese workers, men young
and old who are fluent with their tools,
scraping the bark layer, taking off lengths
to be cleaned and boiled, thin strips
punched for stoppers. It was on that farm
in the heart of Alentejo that I saw your father
and it clicked – how you were fashioned
by your mother and him. And I could see
their four feet, able to breathe and insulated
from cold, cushioned against hard ground.

XYLEM (THE WEIGHT OF LEARNING)

Then the veins in his legs splintered
and his armpit hair turned to grain.
He gasped for breath as gravity
forced him to the carpet. Dog-tired,
his limbs thinned to cabriole.

He found himself on his hands
and knees, his palms flat, his back
straightened out, before balling up,
ten toes curling into lion's claws
until he was a surface, all horizontal.

His rib cage revealed a bevelled edge,
his spine patterned with swirling eyes.
That's when it gathered: the sculptures,
curios and artefacts, the verbs, vocabulary
and glossaries, the encyclopaedic facts.

It would take grown men to lift him
and so they left him. Brushing past,
they recalled just how much he knew,
the table formerly known as boy, took
a damp cloth and wet-wiped the dust.

Bikes become clutter.
Become wondering.
Abandoned saddles. Loose brakes.
Become emails to all the flats
about bikes below getting in the way.
Bikes become no internet.
Become phone calls.
Become engineers.
Bikes become the likelihood
of a pedal or handlebar nobody owns
catching and loosening a cable.
Bikes become an update.
Become a long thread.
Become a four-way exchange.
And more wondering
how nobody's bike wasn't
ridden by anyone
but moved somehow
by someone in a basement
down there for something.
Bikes become displacement.
Become a spray job.
Bikes become bikes that must belong.
Become people moved out years ago.

STORAGE KINGDOM

Mid-morning, I give them a call.
I say, *Is that Carol?* and she says,
No, this is Jade, how can I help you?

I say, *I was thinking of increasing
the size of my space, of upgrading.
The thing is…* and I hear myself

telling Jade the ins and outs of
my predicament, me confiding:
I've tried to condense two units

*and cram everything in but now it's
all squeezed up and if I open the door
I can't get in because of the mattress.*

I ask Jade if she can give me a price
for a bigger unit to move about in
and, can you believe it, she says

*You're in luck, we've got a deal on
a one hundred-and-fifty square foot –*
cheaper than a one hundred unit

and a fifty separate. *Sounds great,*
I say, *cos there's some other crates
at my Mum's down the passage and*

in the box room, at the back of the garage.
I say, *It's not all mine, it belongs to…*
and he… thanks, I'll ring you back, goodbye.

I get to the storage unit ahead of the van from London. They couldn't carry me as a passenger because of insurance. Walking into reception, Carol's sitting behind the desk, eating her lunch out of a Tupperware container. She says sorry between mouthfuls, puts down her fork and swallows, wipes her mouth, says her husband's from New Orleans and does all the cooking. I say, 'Oh, lucky you.' I say, 'So, what's it today?' She says, 'My favourite, prawn jambalaya.'

> Brawn mumble plyer.
> Raw jumble liar.

I sign for a new key, pay for a gold padlock, walk to the bigger unit. Second floor. In a corner. No windows. I pull open the blue metal door, enter the space, breathe in the closed-up air. A message from Steve: they'll be another half hour. I inspect the partition walls, think of going outside but decide to stay with the empty. I need to sit down, use my backpack as a cushion for the concrete, take out my Pret sandwich. It can't compete with prawn jambalaya.

> Yawn rumble gyre.
> Raw jumble liar.

I chew and think of New Orleans. The flooded streets, that storm before Katrina. Checking in at the hotel. The woman on reception informing us the mayor's declared a curfew: twenty-four hours but she cannot promise. The twin room at the rear, the TV greeting us personally. Aircon pumping cold non-stop. News anchors obsessing over landfall. On the single beds in our layers, imagining wrought iron balconies, listening for jazz, ignorant of prawn jambalaya.

> Porn fumble higher.
> Raw jumble liar.

Steve texts. They're here. I go down to meet them. They were forced to go slower than normal. A very heavy load, he was worried for the axles. The back unlatched, they start a human chain passing lidded plastic crates of papers and books from one to the other and onto the trolley. Up to the unit then down again. Until a final crate labelled 'KITCHEN'. Cups, plates, dishes. Stuff too good for charity. When I get home, I'll find the recipe for prawn jambalaya.

> Mourn bumble belier.
> Raw jumble liar.

ALL THE NEVER YOU CAN CARRY

The whole amount of no occasion
that can be lifted and lugged.

Each and every not for a moment
it's feasible to pick up and hump.

The entire lot of in no circumstances
the second person can convey.

Every single no way an individual
is physically capable of carting.

The complete set of not on your life
people in general can schlep.

The parts together of no account
your own self is disposed to shifting.

Or the sum of ain't gonna happen
you guys there are up for grabbing.

HARD DRIVE

our life is out there somewhere
on a hard drive some place
dark and silent deep inside
we are saved we are stored
all we were us recorded
for the time being being ignored

our love is out here somewhere
love that drove us some place
we didn't know we hadn't been
safe and secure behind closed doors
all the files in all the folders
switched off put away

I will get a man to locate our life
to retrieve our life our love
and transfer it so I can relive it
some day our life of years
all the days sitting there
unlooked at us collected

THE SHORTEST DAY

A dark chocolate cake, elegantly displayed,
on an Aubrey Beardsley style vintage plate
by the till in a refurbished coal house café
on the edge of urban wetlands. Where there's
parsnip soup and thick slices of granary bread
for the man who has just ventured inside
to warm himself, after walking the path
that necklaces the inner-city reservoir.

A cold man with a supermarket plastic bag
stuffed inside his jacket pocket, the hole
he's cut with scissors into one of the corners.
An orange plastic bag from the desk drawer
of an upstairs office five miles away, fetched
by another man, suited and softly spoken
who's discreet, keeps a good supply of spares,
advises him on carrying it low to avoid attention.

An orange plastic bag that's full and weighs,
is carried casually, successfully, as though
containing rice or flour or coffee. A bag the man
has been swinging back and forth, back and forth
for half an hour, forty minutes even, longer than
expected, the man, to his relief, not looked at,
not stopped, accused by passers-by, but finding it
physical, the effort needed to make a bag swing.

Swing like incense from an orthodox church
while his legs and feet on autopilot guide him,
glide him around the body of water, its rich border
of reeds and grasses, all biscuit, oatmeal feather,
their dance fashioned by December winds, the bag
buffeted by bluster, bag hitting his knees and shins
as he gets on with swinging, the act of emptying,
happy-go-lucky to those coming the other way.

The everyday swinging of a man wrapped up,
taking in his surroundings, waiting on the spot for
outbreaks of sun, talking aloud, muffled, to someone,
describing a spire in the distance, all the way round
before stopping to turn, head back to the warmth
of the coal house, him arriving shaken out, him
lighter and hungry, denim shins and winter shoes
dusted like icing sugar on a dark chocolate cake.

To dizzywind the ashes
      To kindrelease the ashes
            To roxette the ashes

To lightallow the ashes
      To dayaway the ashes
            To žižek the ashes

To aroseisarose the ashes
      To deruck the ashes
            To nabokov the ashes

To let blendblow the ashes
      To let currentcarry the ashes
            To sufjanstevens the ashes

To let airdance the ashes
      To breezegive the ashes
            To fabriziodeandre the ashes

To unworry the ashes
      To sunsow the ashes
            To susansontag the ashes

To undespair the ashes
      To debonair the ashes
            To flaubert the ashes

To desparple the ashes
      To usheroff the ashes
            To toriamos the ashes

IV. COVERED RESERVOIR

ARCHITECT'S DRAWERS

An office altarpiece. Yours off eBay.
Splintered surface. Two stacked parts.
Three drawers and three drawers

makes six drawers. The first for pins
and staples, a religion of stationery.

The one below, and your collection
of paper, far too good for wrapping –

the hoard of hand-printed sheets,
green-marbled, Italian parchment,
Japanese washi, from that shop

you loved on Southampton Row,
that expensive place you went mad in,

the one you wanted to take me to
so we could choose together.

DESK
after Tusiata Avia

Ask the god to tidy your drawer
neat enough that your life is in order

Ask it to arrange you
Ask it to sort you out

Ruler, stapler
Hole punch, glue

Ask it to stick things back together
Ask it to fasten your days together

Ask the god for right angles
Ask the god for the right angles

Make it straighten stuff
Make it equally measured

Then put your life away
Then close your life

Pig-headed, you refused Berlin and Barcelona,
said *Everyone goes there!* And so, in your obstinacy,
you never gawped at Gaudí, or got to gauge
how they raised up the *Plaza de Toros* in its entirety.
You didn't climb the spiral of the Reichstag's dome.

Now in your passing, I no longer hear you
berate the tourists who go in low-cost droves,
won't ever see you drink in the oldest *Biergarten*,
get a handle on the pils. You weren't that thirsty
and it was all too easy. Let's not even go there.

Like one of Forster's Edwardians, I suppose, high on Highgate
not Fiesole or Rome, you'd put on a funny voice to guarantee
a laugh from me, ask *What on God's earth my dear boy is a 'job'?*

and sometimes, *Oh, do pray tell, what then might a 'weekend' be?*
My educated fellow, in your early thirties and rich with degrees,
on the cusp of it all, with your balms, costly moisturizing creams

I gladly pilfered, and for early balding, that caffeine shampoo.
Like you'd fallen to earth, with no intention of 'earning a living'
by any traditional means, you weren't for the hellish commute,

by no means meant for annual appraisals, scales and increments,
performing unkind, perfunctory tasks, 'stuff that needed doing'.
Being was enough, each day afresh in the freedom of the home,

to collage and create, if and when it pleased you, your leisure
to frame and hang, decorating walls as the mood took or didn't
take you. Shifts, shop work, they were alien to your smooth palms,

your fine piano fingers that had never known the schoolboy stink
of headlines, the weight of a frosted winter morning's broadsheets.
Amid Chopin, *tes petits objets*, a red enamelled pot of beans freshly

ground and filtered, I recall the evening you stopped reading
and from your LRB looked up, in your washed-out denim cut-off
shorts, your woolly socks and Birkenstocks, leapt up the stairs

to find me. I was at the kitchen table, end of term, gone midnight,
stooped over, keying passes and fails into an Excel spreadsheet,
swearing under my breath, pulling my hair out. *What's that word?*

you insisted, as if somehow urgent, *the one for a job that pays well*
but doesn't demand too much thinking, that word for a cushy function,
for comfortable employment with no stress or pressure, looming deadlines,

service that gives a decent wage, a kind of labour, something for a gentleman,
you said it just the other day, like, 'nice work if you can get it'. I said,
Sinecure, you mean sinecure?, my eyes eaten up by the glare of the screen.

CALDO VERDE (SOUP WITH COLLARD GREENS)

Remember stepping off that bus in São Martinho do Porto?
The old lady at the stop. How she led us up the hill to her house,
then took our passports and euros and moved in with her mother.
Eating dinner on the roof beneath the stars, the silence of the sea.

Remember always starting with your caldo verde? Dark green
like seaweed. How on that last evening we poured the rest away
and watched it block the sink. No plunger to hand, how we bought
a product to shift it, emptied the bottle and headed out for a drink.

Remember getting back, going to the kitchen to check on progress?
Finding the pumice eaten away, the metal drain and pipe exposed.
How we covered it with the plastic basin. The old lady next morning
ringing her own bell, and how we pocketed our passports and fled.

Remember running for that train? As it moved through the town,
how we slid down in our seat. How we felt guilty for the old lady,
lived in fear of the old lady. And at dinner parties told the story
of Portugal and of our old lady, you serving up your caldo verde.

REGRET WITH MASSIVE ORANGE, RED AND BROWN KILIM

This morning in the kitchen I was on a roll
getting down in words some mad episode
from way back when I heard a voice it was
Tod he was calling me from the front room
with something about something on TV
I absolutely had to see and *hey!* to come
quick! quick! before it's over and I miss it

like when I was sixteen in love with Paul
Cézanne and watching the holiday show
Dad would call up *Paul, your mountain!*
and I would drop my brush in the water jar
hurry downstairs but I ignored Tod kept on
with what I was in the middle of doing but
he was persistent so it must have been special

Tod wanting me to get up and go find him
and the massive orange, red and brown kilim
I brought back for him from Tbilisi after
I went there for work to interview students
(that took up the whole suitcase meaning
I had to carry my dirty socks and pants
in a plastic carrier bag as hand luggage)

and which folded out to cover the whole
floor of the flat we no longer live in since I
moved out and he wanted to be more central
after all our evenings working away consumed
by own projects own writing when he'd ask me
to come join him plead almost why didn't I
take my stuff through why didn't I join him

CLIMBING TBILISI

Above the brick-domed baths of Abanotubani, rare trees ache with invasion and enemy grab. City spreads, leavened and rising like khachapuri, its rooftops woven, a red and brown kilim. In the butterflied grasses, local teens lie about making out in telescopic view of the billionaire,

his hilltop helipad and gleaming condo rich in the business of balcony. We make fairy steps across the abyss———a slatted bridge that sways, its rusted frame squeaking like the Tin Man, until the dirt path forks and we are drawn by the caw of crows. Homing in, we assume a flock,

but only close-up do we process what cannot take flight: amphibians ample in raucous chorus, the bloated mob stepping over each other. In a raised concrete pond, the frogs are puffed up, crap-loud, a bulbous hubbub of throat-throttle, croaking for a mate and many in swollen song.

We climb the carpet of the museum that's a museum of a museum,
towards the chandelier, amazed our driver, Gaga, whose only
word of English is *Guinness*, has never been. In unheated palace
halls buffed floorboards creak with clipboard hordes doing
gap-fills. Our guide, Tamara, reveals this household name had
high grades, admits he made mistakes, says this and that are true,
that he wrote poems in his youth, and how people still raise a
glass to toast him. I caress a marble door frame, transfer the cold
sheen to my cheek. The walls are crowded with rows of seated,
fur-coated leaders, their smiles and massacre of zeros. Zooming
in on his fat moustache, I think how *gulag* sounds, like *glugging
glue* and *lagging* pipes, admire the gifts kept behind glass: Italian
best wishes, *Ciao Giuseppe,* small red clogs sent from Holland.
Tamara pulls an electric candle out her jacket pocket, lights up the
death mask with a steady flicker. On leaving, we shake Tamara's
hand, give our thanks and compliments, forget to tip her. She
insists we don't miss the green armour-plated Pullman carriage
weighing eighty-three tons, a fact that seems key to remember,
which is when I spot him, the cobbler's son – there up ahead
outside the main municipal building, giant on a plinth, staring on.

Gaga is the diminutive for Giorgi

They estimate that about 1.75 to 2.45 million tonnes of grief enter our system every year. Grief is twice the size of Texas and three times the size of France. As grief is discarded into the environment, its concentration continues to increase. Much of the grief is less dense than joy, meaning it will not sink beneath the appearance of happiness. The strongest, most buoyant grief shows resilience outdoors, allowing it to be transported over far distances. It persists at the surface as you make your way around, carried by currents and gathering, accumulating and forming the Giant Human Patch of Grief. One day all the grief collected enters the gyre. It is unable to leave the area, degrades slowly into small pieces under everyday effects of waves and sun.

All the years close to water. By a bulk of water. That hulk of water. Flat water. Still water. Being water. Water in the dark. Oblivious water. Obviously water. Water where water should be. Water with a roof. With walls. A body of water. Shared water. Everyone's water. Neighbouring water. Neighbourly water. Water with grass on. You couldn't walk on. Water close by. Closed off water. Water behind railings. Water off limits. Supposed water. Ought to be water. Take your word for it water. Water under lock and key. Padlocked water. Water with *Keep Out* signs. Official water. Officious water. Measured water. Metred water. Believed in water. Believed to be water. Hypothetical water. Water waiting. Patient water. Water biding its time. Well-behaved water. Weekday water. Rainy day water. Rained on water. Going nowhere water. Water treading water. Water concealed. Unrevealed. Knew no surprise water. No twilight, sunrise water. No boats or swans water. Nothing floating water. No running on water. Water not sailed on. No kid's laughing water. Water you could land a helicopter on. Take off from. Drown a city with water. Water we presumed to be water. Took for granted water. Ignored for years water. Didn't think twice about water. Blind to water. Could have broken into water. Jumped up and down on water. Hard water. Difficult water. By itself water. A watery self. Water alone. Lonely water. Encased water. With a lid on water. Couldn't breathe water. Or evaporate water. Let off steam water. Dry water. Shy water. Reserved water. Quiet water. Some days not speaking water. Water working. Water not working. Getting worked up water. Water we ran and ran.

HIS NASTURTIUMS / NASTURTIUMS HIM ALWAYS

> funnel-shaped nectar spur / nine paths to the middle
> > hardy / quiet achiever / self-sowing / five sepals

> orange yellow / little trumpets / set singly on their axils
> > happy-go-lucky / in a warm spot / of longish petioles

> ~

rises round / climbs proud / provides support / grows vigorously
> twines / winds roughly about / sweet green / peppery

mustard bright / versatile / low maintenance / good companion
> graces slopes / Saturn smile / adorned / commands attention

> ~

> clumsy / in early summer / unfussy / casual
> > three-carpelled / uppermost / with whorls of unequal

> delicate / parasols / edible / crisp young pods
> > crawling up / thriving / ornamental / trap crop

> ~

easy-going / well-chosen / flat-swirled / blood-stained
> packs a punch / listening in / on a table / well-drained

profuse / surprising / kind to the darkest day
> vibrant stamens / aspiring / waterlily wannabe / at play

> ~

> thriving / wicking away from / transplant shock
> > yield reduced / a June dawn / a first frost frisks

> *stun of turista / tsunami of tint / taunting untrim*
> > *saintly truant / satin arms / run riot in autumn ruins*

BOY AT THE END OF A LONG NARROW GARDEN

See how the boy sits, slim on a rotten wooden chair that's just about standing. There, he just about sits at the end of a long narrow garden of hard clay soil, the lawn of scrappy grass that gently climbs. From the end he surveys the rear of the red-bricked terraced house he lives in. He sits by day with distance and sky and often now, when the wooden chair permits, sits on into the night.

There are people in the house, his house, people in the kitchen whose back door opens out onto steps leading down to a yard and long narrow garden. He sits, boy-like, there at the end of the garden, his garden, in the company of foxgloves that love the dim light and damp, thrive in the partial shade of the neighbours' mature trees, sycamores in full leaf, on either side closing in.

Bodies are moving within the backdoor's frame, people talking in the house, but the foxgloves are quiet in the garden as he sits on the rotten wooden chair he carried to the end, precariously, and sometimes a fox. Between the low slat fences and tall stems of pink and purple hoods, and the bees, behind a glossy screen of shrubs, the tower of summer lilac at the end of the garden, he sits.

With a feint-ruled notebook and pen to hand, a can of warm cider by his feet, at the very far end of a long narrow lawned garden the boy writes, writing words that are legible only to him. He writes as he sits, sitting out the summer with himself, by himself, just about him. The people, all the people, he opened the door when the doorbell rang and, one after another, they let themselves in.

HAND PUPPETS (YOU AT YOUR YOUEST)

Whenever I stop and think of you at your youest,
the nights are drawing in and we're both at home
in our two-bed rented flat on Mount View Road.
You're in the front room and I'm in the kitchen.

Behind me, the giant poster of *Kikker in de Wolken* –
Frog in the Clouds, announcing a children's play
at Maastricht's Vrijthof theatre. It takes up the wall.
We had glass cut and carried it back, thin but heavy.

I'm working away when, I don't know what it is –
a reflection in the laptop screen or small movement,
something in the corner of my eye. I turn my head
and there in the doorway, halfway up the frame,

I've a visitor – Turtle or Mouse – peering round,
come to see me. Turtle, his long neck and round beak,
Mouse, his whiskers sniffing the evening air. I say,
Hey there, how are you doing? What are you up to?

I lean forward in my chair, shift to catch sight of you –
you of the hand, you of the arm, you of the face
lit up behind the wall. I can see you – when you were
you at your youest and we were us, in good hands.

V. INTENTIONS

LOVING THE SOCIAL ANTHROPOLOGIST I
Romania

He was off doing fieldwork, gone weeks on end,
studying the young men who'd fled to Spain
for work, a rite of passage. What did it mean
for the mothers and sisters and wives left behind
in the emptied out towns of Transylvania?

He collected me in Budapest. I don't recall much:
the parliament, and some party in a bar in the park
to celebrate Mr. Gay Hungary (led there by the friend
of a friend, a ballet dancer we were crashing with),
eight flat hours by train across plains to Romania.

*

Cluj-Napoca was his base. It was arty and buzzing
and I was in his hands. He spoke the language well,
had the weekend planned. We downed shots of țuică
and I abandoned myself in his rented room, next day
wound through his ravines, his canyons and mountains.

We stopped a night in Baia Mare, had cheap and tasty
pizza and wine. It must have been the randomness
of the place, the fact he was ordering that made me hungry.
I heard his 'da, da…' and his 'vă rog', his 'mulțumesc',
watched him nod to the waitress as he chose my topping.

*

In Sighet, on the border with Ukraine, he ran in the mud
from bus to bus to find ours for the Merry Cemetery.
Sitting in the open back, he chatted to the farmhands.
The snow was waist high, and I lost him a while as we
took in the bright blue wooden tombstones. Săpânța blue.

He translated for me: the man who fell in front of a train,
the three-year old girl hit by a taxi outside her house,
the mother-in-law you mustn't wake in case she bites you.
The accidents, final moments, all shown with cheer,
carving fun out of death with gloss paint and rhyme.

WHEN WE WERE JACKSON POLLOCK

Screwdriver to hand   you prised open   our colours   the little tins
   of gloss and matt   not thinking   for a moment   or holding back
diving in   dripping viscous   leaning over   bare surface
   me circling above   teasing thick   liquid to dance   away and off

   flicked flicked flicked   our brushes   far across wanting
we   something elemental   to take over us
   inviting confusion   you hovered   dribbled   splat   layering
languorous   your lines longing   winding tangling doing   their own thing   fast

welcoming the random   rhythm feeling bolder   fluid spilling
and spooling   around along   two men filling   a stretch of blank
   nothing intended   no shapes   no forms   we could make out
sky blue mint green   red white black   our canvas chaos   left outside

that summer that somehow   fixed and dried   didn't run or bleed   could we believe
   so you and me might   stand it upright   hang the dizzy   drips and flicks
to fill a wall   ceiling to floor   with the now   the instant
   being taken by   the automatic   the unthinkingness   of us

I CAN BE HAPPILY

engrossed in some
        have my head stuck in
looking out at the
        noticing the new

admiring the curve of
        fixed on the way a
lost in the recent
        and oblivious to

I can be enjoying a quiet
        browsing the latest
choosing between
        or flicking through

taking in all the
        catching up on my
touching base with
        planning an overdue

I can be peering over at
        preparing a small
getting ready for
        in the queue

looking forward to a
        when suddenly I
out of nowhere
        picture you

Gone midnight, half-listening to Justin Bieber when he
stops singing. A man starts speaking, *You may be 38 years old
as I happen to be. And one day, some great opportunity stands
before you.* My ears prick up because you were 38 and
it sounds like Martin Luther King. What opportunity?

Justin's back. I think it's 'Yummy', the one that goes
You got that yummy-yum, that yummy-yummy and I am
wondering if I just imagined it, or if it was an advert,
and if so, what Martin Luther King is advertising,
I mean, what Martin Luther King is being used for.

Curious, I google 'Martin Luther King 38'. It brings up
his appeal *to stand up for some great principle, some great issue,
some great cause,* though as I'm reading Justin's lovesick,
Oh-oh-oh-whoa, Oh, I'll be fucked up if you can't be right here.
I still can't make the link, type 'Bieber Luther King'.

First up is *Rolling Stone* magazine with '*Justin Bieber
Addresses Martin Luther King Jr. Sample Controversy.*'
Bieber used Luther King's sermon on his album *Justice,*
was forced to make a public apology. Wikipedia tells me
Luther King died at 39, his *because you are afraid* speech

a year before his assassination. *Life begins at forty* they say
but preacher, popstar, or PhD, it doesn't for everyone.
You'd be 44. They say lots of things. I press pause,
look up from my laptop and the moon comes out. I sit,
try to remember where I was, what I was half-doing.

ON MAILING A LOCK OF HIS HAIR TO AMERICA, BELATEDLY

Would his hair be worth it?
Would his hair provide comfort?
Would his hair cause upset?
Would his hair be an act of violence?
Would his hair destroy their day?

Would his hair survive the journey?
Would his hair have to declare itself?
Would his hair be seized?
Would his hair still shine?
Would his hair be hair after all this time?

CHECKING IN

May is your birthday
so we send messages
of good wishes and share
how spring is coming on,
which fruit and vegetables
are showing promise
in the raised beds.
Your mother tells me
about the latest display
of antiques, of her turn
at the collectibles co-op
up at Forest Farm, how
she always includes
an item of yours.
Last time was vintage
Bakelite trucks and cars,
the hardened resin
a revolution, today
highly collectible.
She says your Dad is still
happy to have retired but
likes to keep his hand
in with the faculty.
June is when you died
so we're in touch again,
usually a short note.
July was the cremation,
which we let go unspoken.
We say what we have to
when we have to,
most words in early May.

Autumn again. And I've been thinking about Pennsylvania. The trees, the leaves and your parents on the porch overlooking the yard. Like this time last year, when autumn came, and I got to thinking about Pennsylvania, its trees, their leaves, the technicolor, and your mother and father, together on a warm September morning on the porch overlooking the yard. When I say autumn, I mean fall. The sight of fall and the thought of it all, all those reds, oranges, yellows and pinks. How many falls since my first thoughts of going? Since those first ought-to-go's came into my head? Each year my thinking brightens, until the thoughts begin to dry out and brown and one by one, start falling.

> You drove me
>> in their old Volvo
> through the Appalachians
>> and in the Foster Joseph Sayers
>>> reservoir we swam.

> We left the car
>> and in the darkening
> depths of Bald Eagle Forest
>> got caught out – the two of us
>>> soaked against a trunk.

LOVING THE SOCIAL ANTHROPOLOGIST II
Almería

His country was hot,
his economy informal.
His method was covert –
participant observation.

Before dawn in the square,
he would watch the men gather
collecting in shadows
and concentric circles –

the lightest in the middle,
the darkest around the edges.
Some were chosen, loaded
into vans and driven off.

To rip off plastic sheeting.
To lay on plastic sheeting.
For tomatoes and aubergines,
cucumbers, peppers.

He said the greenhouses
could be seen from space.
He said that by sunrise
the men were invisible.

NURTURE

I was raised as a tomato in a tomato shaped house.
My bedroom walls were tomato red, the carpet too.

I was shy, didn't play much with the other tomatoes
and locked myself away cataloguing my tomatoes.

I spent what little pocket money I had on tomatoes,
most evenings watched tomatoes for hours on end.

Mum was half Tomato. Sundays she'd iron my tomato.
My packed lunch was tomato ketchup sandwiches.

Weekdays, I'd run and catch an early tomato.
My favourite subject was Tomato. I was good at it.

A small-sized tomato, other tomatoes bruised me
for being a bright tomato. Sad, unhappy tomato.

The careers officer planted a seed inside my head:
to work hard and become a professional tomato.

So I went to Tomato University, took a joint degree,
majoring in Tomato but with a minor in Tomatoes.

There were so many tomatoes, some sour and green,
but one ripe and blush tomato – I wanted to eat it.

A well-rounded tomato, sweet sense of humour,
origin the United States of Tomato. Beefsteak.

We rented a tomato and filled it with tomatoes,
collected rare tomatoes and placed them on a shelf.

Weekends when we weren't training our tomatoes,
we'd go on excursions, walk around old tomatoes.

If our tomatoes were flat, we'd pump them up.
Tomatoes flew. We deepened in colour, made soup.

WE WEREN'T MARRIED. HE WAS MY CIVIL PARTNER.

By which I mean in the past.
By which I mean mine, belonging to me.
By which I mean one night came into my life.
By which I mean boyfriend.
By which I mean lover.

By which I mean with time, significant other.
By which I mean partner.
By which I mean serious undertaking with another person.
By which I mean another man.
By which I mean men.

By which I mean two consenting adults.
By which I mean same-sex.
By which I mean sex.
By which I mean exploring sex.
By which I mean sometimes great, sometimes samey.

By which I mean civil, courteous, polite and kind.
By which I mean officially, in November 2009.
By which I mean a registry office.
By which I mean two witnesses.
By which I mean the payment of thirty-five pounds.

By which I mean a blazer and tie.
By which I mean bothering to iron a shirt.
By which I mean bringing a CD along with a favourite song.
By which I mean holding hands.
By which I mean a quick, embarrassed kiss.

By which I mean two quick, deserving pints.
By which I mean back into our jeans and off on our bikes.
By which I mean on with our lives.
By which I mean I'm still alive.
By which I mean *I do*.

ST. PANCRAS

'I want my time with you'
Tracey Emin

I want my time with you
            for a coffee in St. Pancras.

I wanted my time with you
            over coffees in St. Pancras.

I wasted my time with you
            during coffee in St. Pancras.

I fasted my time with you
            sipping coffee in St. Pancras.

Fast was my time with you,
            quick coffees in St. Pancras.

Fate was my time with you:
            the last coffee in St. Pancras.

GRIEF AS NORTHERN FRENCH LANDSCAPE
Lille–Paris

It sits there.
Like a slag heap
taking years to settle.

Black pyramids into the distance,
their covering of stubborn
vegetation.

First bushes, then apple trees
from the chucked cores
of miners' lunches.

Even alpine plants
whose seeds hitched a lift
on the wood used for pit props.

It appears, all a blur,
through the double-glazed
window of a high-speed train.

Forward-facing, I glide down
the straights and curves
of track we knew,

fast, from the industrial heart,
south to the City of Lights
where I met you, where I meet you.

THE ONCE-A-MONTH NIGHT

I didn't sit with Joe in a college bar
to hear him whining on – over wine
that he'd never meet someone. It was beer.

He didn't say, *Won't you come with me?*
or insist, come closing time, *Go on, please!*
I said, *No, go by yourself, I'm not comfortable.*

We didn't go, didn't queue, didn't pay.
There was no music. It wasn't disco and so
I wouldn't venture into the blackness

or turn my back to find Joe gone.
Joe clung to me, not fussed, a wallflower
in his sweet scent of Clinique *Happy.*

I didn't drink or scour, but bottled it,
not managing to find my body
dancing towards you. You were standing still.

And no, you didn't tell me I kissed too hard
because I didn't kiss you, never knew
inside the dry ice that you were even there.

The dawn never came. We didn't amble
home with your girlfriends as chaperones –
they saw me and, frankly, did not approve.

We didn't date, check to see if we'd fit together.
Each of us went on to travel nowhere.
I met nobody, lived thirteen years alone.

and I should be breaking

having a complete

be saying please ignore

should be it's fine

be don't worry about

and raising a

should be talking with

for old time's

should be if only

be lighting a

should be can't quite

be he'd want me to

should be it's all so

should be taking a

in a flood of

and having to find some

I'm being

really I'm

didn't see that

grateful for what we

talking over

be life teaches

if I could somehow

sitting in a calm

be grasp how

know he'd want me

still so

making a   about getting

welling

thank you

it's just that my

and will be   spending a quiet

just when you least

moments where we

reliving the many

does make you more

no point in trying

thinking of the first

quickly passes

to

so

and I don't even

and holding

VI. ATTACHMENT

YOUR BRAIN
after Layli Long Soldier

Your brain weighs ██ grams. Your brain weighed ██ grams.

Your brain was weighed on the ██ of ██ 2016. Your brain was weighed three days after you died. You died on or about the ██ of ██.

A post-mortem took place at ███████████████
██████████████. It was carried out on the instructions of H. M. Coroner for ███████ London.

The post mortem reference code was TS/PM/F21/16. This was not the code. I made it up, but it looked similar.

The report was completed on the ███████ of ██ 2016. That was seven weeks after you died.

The post-mortem was held because there was an inquest. There was an inquest because you were a young man and to die so young is unusual.

In email correspondence with the coroner's office they used the term *investigation*. The investigation *touching* your death. Your death was touched by an investigation.

The investigation reference code was 3478/34/TBX. This was not the code. I made it up, but it looked similar.

The initials stood for the woman case officer. I don't know what the numbers mean.

Another term for post-mortem is *autopsy*. Autopsy is used more commonly in America. Your brain was from America. An overseas brain.

But back to the weight of your brain. One and half kilos, give or take a gram.

Brains are not metric but biological, physical. Brains grow with schooling.

Your brain had degrees, a scholarship to come here. A musical brain that learnt a little Chopin. A bemused by Kim Jong-Il brain.

A culinary brain that loved to cook: Toulouse sausages, Le Puy green lentils. From the south-west. Where we went by train. With our backpacks and our brains.

In French, brain is masculine, *le cerveau*. I see the 'cer' of *cerise* and 'veau' of *veal*. Brain: cherry-veal. That's how I shall think of it from now on.

And there's water in the French for brain. You must see the *eau*.

Water on the brain can be harmful. An excessive accumulation of cerebrospinal fluid results in a condition known as *hydrocephalus*.

Your brain was fine. The right amount of water. A well-hydrated brain. One with many regions. My favourites were: medulla, cerebellum, pallia, pons.

Especially pons. Like the Catalan film director Ventura Pons, his film about the long-serving woman forced to take a holiday from her job selling tickets at the local cinema, only to return a week later to find it gone. Demolished. We saw it, enjoyed it, one Sunday evening in Madrid. *Anita no perd el tren. Anita Takes a Chance* seemed an odd translation.

Your brain hated holidays, annoyed by the break to its routine, put out by the pointless rupture to your writing.

Pons has adapted work by other writers: *What's It All About, Idiot Love, Caresses, To Die (or Not)*. Did we see those? Should we have seen them?

I liked your medulla, i.e. the marrow. Also the title of Bjørk's fifth album, almost entirely *a capella*. You didn't rate her, would sing shrill ...*in a hidden place!* to imitate her.

Then there was your hippocampus and basal ganglia, your optic tectum that helped you see. See films, like the one above with me. I was fond of your thalamus and hypothalamus, your olfactory bulb, your perfume.

Each region had its function. The prefrontal cortex carried out your planning and working memory, your motivation, attention, executive control.

Let's start with planning: I didn't plan any of this and nor did you.

My memory works everyday remembering. I am motivated to not forget. I am attentive to fix you in *my* brain. I am an executor. I took control.

I like being in control. You might call me a *control freak*. I would understand. This was out of my control.

Maybe it was in my control, but I didn't pay attention to what was happening. Maybe my motivation was to look away.

To block out your brain, its complex web of interconnections.

There are a few areas where neurons continue to be generated. Those present in your early childhood are basically the same as in adult life.

Your adult life was shorter than it should have been.

Your childhood neurons came from Eugene, Oregon. Eugene, Oregon: an anagram of *gene* and *neuron*.

Your brain was provided with so much information, about head orientation and limb position, the chemical composition of the blood stream.

And about the temperature and atmosphere, sound and light.

Like the light through the back door window. Crouch Hill. Our raised ground floor flat. The sun rays streaming in.

Your brain processed the sound of those raucous jays on heavy summer days.

Days when we'd sit on the back step at the top of the iron stairs down into the garden and you'd tilt your brain and rest it on my right shoulder, wrap an arm around my neck to calm me, lower my pulse.

Motor systems enabled your body movements, put your muscles in motion. Muscles in that wrapping arm, that tilting brain.

At the lowest level, motor areas in the medulla and pons controlled *stereotyped movements* such as walking, breathing, swallowing. I never thought your movements were stereotyped.

Your movements belonged uniquely to you. Your gait. Walking gaily. Breathing at will. Swallowing coffee, wine, whatever I told you.

In the midbrain was the red nucleus, coordinating movements of your arms and legs.

How I watched your legs and how they swung, how your brain made them swing. Back and forth, up and down, pushing down on the garden fork, digging.

Red nucleus. Red like the harissa in your chicken, cooked in the orange cast iron casserole I bought at the *braderie* in Lille for just two euros. The bargain that fed us.

Fed us beneath those coloured German pub lights strung through the branches of the trees. Red, blue, yellow, green. Red, blue, yellow, green.

Lights that stayed out when it started to rain. And we ran inside with our brains.

Dry brains, drunk brains, that jumped around and danced.

And how your brain let your legs dance, how they danced that first night as legs like to.

Danced on that dancefloor where my brain manoeuvred me, so I had no choice but to dance towards you.

~~I wrote 'Your Brain' in two goes.~~
~~The second go was in Glasgow.~~
~~I wrote most of it before I got there.~~
~~Most of the poem wasn't written in Glasgow.~~
~~I had to the finish the beginning of the poem.~~
~~I needed specific details for the poem.~~
~~I added in the details in a café on the Byres Road.~~

The Byres Road was a short walk from the university.
The café receipt indicated I was served by 'Danny'.
Danny was friendly and Italian from his accent.
I had the savoury tart because they'd run out of summer salad.
The total came to £13.55 with a fresh juice and espresso.
The café was modern and looked vegetarian.
The café had the pervasive smell of bacon.
It was lunch break from the conference.
The bi-annual conference of the Association of European Studies.
I couldn't decide what to attend or where to go.
It was after one o'clock and I'd travelled on my own.
It was large and anonymous and full of American scholars.
I talked to a man behind a stand promoting 'Scotland in Europe'.
They hadn't organised any receptions or a conference dinner.
No wine for free. No events being sponsored.
Eduroam didn't work. I couldn't log on.
My username that day was 'tangerine416'.
My password was 'pineapple175'.
I wasn't presenting that day.
I was the discussant in a panel on accountability.

~~I was prepared for once and had made decent notes.~~
~~The first page of the poem was more difficult.~~
~~I didn't know if I should use the details.~~
~~I knew the details could be found in an attachment.~~

I knew the email was sent a year ago.
I knew the month of the message.
I'd have to trawl through my folder called 'Tod' to find it.
I wasn't sure if I should open the message.
I wasn't sure if I could read the message. Again.
I didn't know if I could open the attachment in the café.
I didn't know if I could read the attachment. Again.
I had once opened and read the attachment.
It was a small serving, and I was disappointed.
I decided to try to open it casually.
I ate it and was still hungry. I told myself it was healthy.
I told myself if was good to be hungry.
I scrolled and scanned for the detail.
Then I pressed X on the tab and the attachment disappeared.

WRITING TO YOUR MOTHER

Whenever I sit down to write to your mother
there's the question of you,
and whenever you come into my head
there's the decision to be made
whether or not to mention your name.

Whenever I go to mention your name
it's another reminder you've gone
and whenever your *goneness* seems violent
and I recall your mother will be reading my words
I search for something more upbeat.

Whenever I start searching for what's upbeat
I end up mining for a funny episode,
an anecdote, falling back on your silliness,
and see your mother's eyes passing over my words,
her mouth turning up at the edges.

Whenever your mother's mouth turns up at the edges
she's using the many muscles it takes to smile
and in the process, that small smile
may fool her into thinking she is living
a moment of happiness.

FIRST DRAFTS

It was early May
and I hadn't done with April.
April was still there,
lingering with its words,
thousands of them,
titles, sections, paragraphs.

All that April formatting,
that incorrect formatting,
the misspellings and indents,
the needless tabs.

It had been hot
but I hadn't felt it.
So many different greens.
Never saw them.
Cherry blossom all over the place,
apparently.

How April clung on,
persistent
with obligations.
It was early May. Rain.

PUTTING IT OUT THERE

So here I am worrying myself to death
about commodifying your death,
arranging and sequencing your death,
curating the left and right pages of your death.
deciding which parts of your death to leave out.

Here I am again, giving a title to your death,
choosing an attractive cover for your death,
(will your death have French flaps?)
writing intelligent-sounding blurb for your death,
thinking how we might best promote your death,
who might best be willing to endorse it.

Still me, waiting to be sent a proof of your death.
I'll need an eye for detail to check your death for typos.
I've got to get it right – the finger-feel,
the texture of the paper of the pages of your death,
ensure a sharp jet black for your death's ink.
(I'm wondering about the numbers in your death's ISBN).

Before I sign off on your death – your death done,
and wait for a box with hard copies of your death
and organize things to launch your death – finally,
then wait, for reviews of your death (hopefully considered),
to be told how well your death has sold.

SNOWDROPS / DROPBOX

those first shoots   like blank sheets
I save them   with my eyes

morning white   pages bright
give each a name   done wintering

*   *

their talent for   face down
silent gathering   of the gallant

I file them   their torrent
in folders   of a cloud

inside the folds of   my springing brain
each year   retrieved renewed

*   *

grateful for   space freed
green marking   leaves

days ordered   modified restored
me opened   this latest version

STARCHITECT (2016)

He was my air-punching Alpha Centaurian, my bama and shaka,
my basic wage answer book, my bish-bash-bosh, my bodhi tree,
    my bovver, my bro-hug.

He was my centredness, my chargrill, my deffo flauta, my glamping jackalope,
my go ba, my hackable sensi, my human bean, my krump lamellophone,
    my left justification, my right justification.

He was my likembe, my likeliest parmp, my listicle, my long-running maitake,
my play-to-play mofongo, my refleet, my Scooby Snack,
    my self-selected right-footer, my sleepsuit, my snus.

He was my softscape, my splendiferous sense, my starter marriage,
my startfulmood tink, my stratum corneum, my test drive,
    my top gun, my vlog, my yogalate.

GRIEF AS THE PREAMBLE OF THE MAASTRICHT TREATY

HIS MAJESTY THE KING OF SHOCK,

HER MAJESTY THE QUEEN OF DENIAL,

THE PRESIDENT OF THE FEDERAL REPUBLIC OF
REFUSAL,

THE PRESIDENT OF THE PAIN REPUBLIC,

HIS MAJESTY THE KING OF GUILT,

THE PRESIDENT OF THE ANGER REPUBLIC,

THE PRESIDENT OF DEPRESSION,

THE PRESIDENT OF THE UPWARD TURN REPUBLIC,

HIS ROYAL HIGHNESS THE GRAND DUKE OF
RECONSTRUCTION,

HER MAJESTY THE QUEEN OF WORKING THROUGH,

THE PRESIDENT OF THE REPUBLIC OF ACCEPTANCE,

HER MAJESTY THE QUEEN OF THE UNITED KINGDOM OF
HOPE AND FUTURE,

RESOLVED to mark a new stage in the process of living,

RECALLING the historic importance of us,

CONFIRMING their attachment to the principles of love, friendship,
and companionship,

DESIRING to deepen the memory of what they shared for a while,

DESIRING to enhance self-functioning in the absence of the other,

RESOLVED to achieve the strength and resilience of body and mind,

DETERMINED to promote remembrance, acceptance, and self-forgiveness,

RESOLVED to establish a day-to-day routine as part of coping,

RESOLVED to implement a policy of continuation in order to promote peace of mind, anxiety reduction and sleep,

REAFFIRMING their objective to facilitate the free movement of the individual indoors and out, while ensuring the safety and security of the individual without hijack by sudden emotion or temporary breakdown,

RESOLVED to maintain a close union between the living and the dead, whereby the living can make decisions regarding the dead step-by-step in accordance with the principles of time, distance, and incremental progress,

IN VIEW of steps to be taken in order to advance individual restoration,

HAVE DECIDED to establish Grief and to this end have designated as their plenipotentiaries:

PAUL STEPHENSON, Minister for Sadness

PAUL STEPHENSON, Minister for Wallowing

PAUL STEPHENSON, Minister for Excessive Drinking

PAUL STEPHENSON, Minister for Going Round in Circles

PAUL STEPHENSON, Minister for Regret and If Only

PAUL STEPHENSON, Minister for Sleeping In

PAUL STEPHENSON, Minister for Old Photos

PAUL STEPHENSON, Minister for Holding Onto and Hoarding

PAUL STEPHENSON, Minister for Storage Units

PAUL STEPHENSON, Minister for Replaying and Replaying the Past

PAUL STEPHENSON, Minister for Ruminating and Writing

PAUL STEPHENSON, Minister for Not Letting Go or Moving On

WHO, having exchanged their full powers, found in good and due form, have agreed as follows:

TITLE I

COMMON PROVISIONS

Article A

By this Treaty, the HIGH CONTRACTING PARTIES establish among themselves a GRIEF UNION, hereinafter called 'the Union'.

This Treaty marks a new stage in the process of maintaining a close union between the living and the dead with a view to celebrating the past without due hindrance to the present and with a commitment to reconstruction and to the moving forwards towards a future, to be negotiated by the High Contracting Parties.

[TRUNCATED]

WEDDING IN LIMOUSIN

I'm writing this in the swimming pool,
in a swimming pool in which I am
the only swimmer. I have stopped
swimming to write this poem, here alone,

just arrived, my first swim. Three trains
and a taxi, 38 degrees, a June heatwave.
Standing here, cooling off, the robot
cleaning underwater, almost company.

A pen is letting out its ink, a notebook
covered in wet patches from my wet arm,
right arm, right hand. Blotched words.
Sun. Sun hot on my back, the blanks

of paper wrinkling into waves. France.
Sound of a tractor and a moment ago
church bells. A breeze, honeysuckle.
All this way. I have come to represent you

but I'm also here for me. Hey, a swallow
just skimmed the pool, was off again.
Sixth in a row. A swallow for each year
you've been gone. It's time to swim.

ACKNOWLEDGEMENTS

Some of these poems have been published in poetry journals and anthologies: *14 Magazine, Acumen, Atrium, Bad Lilies, Dust Poetry Magazine, Fenland Poetry Journal, Finished Creatures, Fragmented Voices, Free Verse, Ink, Sweat & Tears, Irisi, Live Canon Poetry Competition Anthology, London Grip, Long Poem Magazine, Madrigal, Magma, Oxford Poetry, Oxford Review of Books, Poetry Wales, Propel, Raceme, The Alchemy Spoon, The French Literary Review, The Friday Poem, The Frogmore Papers, The High Window, The Interpreter's House, The Kindling, The Moth, The North, The Pomegranate, The Rialto, Under the Radar, Wet Grain, Wild Court, Winchester Poetry Prize Anthology.*

'One year on' was the winner of the Free Verse Poetry Book Fair poetry competition 2017 judged by Daljit Nagra. 'The Once-a-Month Night' was highly commended by Seán Hewitt in the Poets and Players poetry competition 2021. 'Birkenstocks' was commended by Andrew McMillan in the Winchester Poetry Prize 2020. 'Boy at the End of a Long Narrow Garden' was longlisted in the Live Canon International Poetry Competition 2020. 'Grief as the Preamble of the Maastricht Treaty' was longlisted in the Live Canon International Poetry Competition 2022.

My thanks to everyone who has supported my writing from early on. I am very grateful to all the poets, administrators, event organisers and promoters from the Jerwood/Arvon mentoring scheme, Aldeburgh Eight, Poetry Business Writing School, Coffee-House Poetry at the Troubadour, the Poetry School and Manchester Writing School. Thanks too to Helena Nelson, and Peter and Ann Sansom, who have been a constant source of inspiration and advice. Thanks also to the Poetry in Aldeburgh team, their energy and enthusiasm. A massive thanks for the good company and guidance of brilliant poet friends in the Panton Arms group in Cambridge, and The Lambs in London.

Enormous thanks to everyone who has helped shape this collection. Thank you to David Tait, Elisabeth Sennitt Clough and Jean Sprackland for comments on very early poems. Love and thanks to my Saturday morning online collective (Kathy Pimlott, Pam Thompson, Ramona Herdman, Fokkina McDonnell, Sarah Mnatzaganian) who helped me through the lockdowns and commented so astutely on many of the poems, and which are so much tighter as a result. Thanks to all the poetry editors who have engaged so attentively with the poems as they have been published in magazines. Thanks also to the Poetry School and The Poetry Business, and to their tutors including Kathryn Simmonds and Will Harris, and to Jonathan Catherall at Tentacular. Credit: J. Bieber, lyrics 'Yummy' and 'Stay'.

My thanks to Lisa Kelly, Matt Howard and Ricardo Bloch for their thoughts and perceptive comments. A huge thanks to Jan Heritage for her close-up reading of the manuscript around the lesser known islands of Greece, and to Susannah Hart for the meticulous proof-reading. Thank you to Jean Hall and Audrey Ardern-Jones for their continued belief in my writing. Eternal gratitude to Jean for such generous friendship, particularly on the difficult days. My thanks for driving me and putting me up – several of the poems could not have happened without her.

My sincere gratitude to John McAuliffe for his sensitive reading and editing, and to Michael Schmidt, Jazmine Linklater, Andrew Latimer and all at Carcanet for their detailed work on the book. For their generous endorsements, I'm grateful to Seán Hewitt, Niall Campbell, Jonathan Edwards and Penelope Shuttle.

Love and thanks to my family, Tod's family, and our common friends. Love and thanks to Scott for his support and companionship throughout. Thanks to Cambridge and Brussels friends. Thanks to poetry and to all the poets, for the friendship and strength they continue to give me.